KidLit-O .

Career As A Veterinarian

What They Do, How to Become One, and

What the Future Holds!

Brian Rogers

KidLit-O Books

www.kidlito.com

Cover lamge © Andres Rodriguez - Fotolia.com

Table of Contents

About KidCaps

KidLit-O is an imprint of BookCaps™ that is just for kids! Each month BookCaps will be releasing several books in this exciting imprint. Visit are website or like us on Facebook to see more!

A veterinarian working with a patient[1]

---

[1] Image source: http://topcollegesonline.org/how-to-become-a-veterinarian/

Introduction

It was the last thing that Susan Bianucci expected to see. She was in her car, driving along Maybank Highway in South Carolina, when she spotted an abandoned dog on the side of the road. The poor little dog was so dehydrated and underfed that it could barely stand up as the big cars and trucks drove by. Because Susan's husband was a veterinarian and founder of Veterinary Specialty Care, an animal hospital that was staffed with several qualified surgeons and animal doctors, she felt that it was her job to help any sick animal that she came across.

Susan pulled to the side of the road and picked up the little dog, who only weighed 29 pounds (about half of what it should have weighed). She took the little dog to her husband's clinic, where they decided to try and help it get healthy again. After giving the dog fluids and some food, the medical team decided to perform a special surgery to help get rid of some cancerous tumors in its body. Imagine the surprise of the team as they watched the sick little female dog (whom they had named Maisey) recovered well and started to gain weight. It wasn't long before she weighed 52 pounds and was cancer free. Maisey was soon adopted by one of the surgery technicians who worked on her and went on to live a life filled with lots of love from her new family.

How did Susan's husband, Doctor Bianucci, feel about his time treating Maisey? He said, "It is impossible to describe what a sweet dog [Maisey] was." In fact, on another occasion Doctor Bianucci described the overall joy that he feels when working with animals: "God has given me the gift of being able to make a living doing what I love."[2]

Have you ever imagined what it would be like to be able to have a job like Doctor Bianucci where you can save the life of a sick animal or to help find a loving home for a pet that doesn't have one? Would you like to spend each day making sure that the animals in your community are happy and disease-free? If so, then the career of a veterinarian might just be the career for you! In this exciting handbook, we will be learning all about who veterinarians are and what they do. What would you most like to learn about this fascinating career?

We will divide up our consideration into seven gripping sections, each one looking at a different part of being a veterinarian. The first section will tell us what veterinarians do with their time at work and what different kinds of veterinarians you can expect to see. We will also see the oath that all veterinarians take after they finish school

2 Quotation sources: http://veterinaryspecialtycare.com

and the amount of money that an average veterinarian makes.

The second section will show us what the training is like to become a veterinarian (also called a "vet"). After finishing their studies at a four-year college, did you know that future vets have to go to medical school, just like doctors who work with human patients? Although doctors who work with humans and doctors who work with animals learn different subjects in their classes, we will see that both careers mean a lot of studying and taking lots of tests.

The third section will answer the question: "Is being a vet an easy job?" As you can probably imagine, the answer is "no". Being a vet has some truly unique challenges each and every day. From the types of animals that they work with to the schedule that they have to keep, a lot is expected of a vet and sometimes it seems like there just aren't enough hours in the day to accomplish everything that they want to. Despite all the challenges, however, veterinarians truly love what they do.

The fourth section will show us what the average day of work is like for a veterinarian. We will get to look over the shoulder of a vet to see how they spend their time at their place of work. Would you be surprised to know that, just like any other doctor, a vet must divide their time between handling emergencies, visiting patients, researching, performing surgeries, and talking with family members of the patient? We will also see how a vet's workday isn't necessarily over once they go home.

The fifth section of this handbook will tell us what the hardest part of being a veterinarian is. While the training can be difficult at times and both the pressure and schedule can be hard for some people to handle, the hardest part of being a vet has to do with something that the vet has no control over – how the animals they treat react to the care they receive.

The sixth section will talk about what the future holds for veterinarians. We will see whether or not there will be lots of jobs available in about ten years or so and what kinds of new technologies will be available to help vets be even more effective at their jobs.

Finally, the seventh section will tell you what you can do right now to get ready to be a veterinarian. Even though you may still have to wait a few years before going to college and then to veterinary school, there are some fundamental qualities and skills that you can learn right now that will help you to be a good vet. Try and see which ones you need to work on the most.

Veterinarians the world over help our pets to stay healthy and keep animals in the community free of disease and injuries. They play a hugely important role in the country, and we can be thankful that these intelligent men and women have chosen this career. Are you ready to learn more about the job of a veterinarian and about the people who have chosen it? Then let's get started with the first section.

Chapter 1: What is a veterinarian?

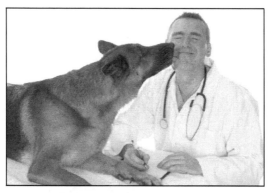

A happy patient says "thank you" to its doctor[3]

As you probably know, a vet is a doctor whose patients are animals, and maybe you have even visited a vet yourself when your pet got sick. But did you know that veterinarians don't only work with dogs and cats? There are vets who work with large animals, vets who work in the military,

[3] Image source: http://www.coolcitydogs.com/veterinarian-tested-and-approved

and vets who work at zoos. In this section, we will have a look at all the different kinds of vets that you can expect to meet someday. We will also see the oath that every single veterinarian must take.

Let's start with the veterinarian that you have probably visited personally – the kind that takes care of household pets and works in a **small clinic**. These kinds of vets treat sick dogs, cats, birds, lizards, gerbils, hamsters, rabbits, and even snakes. They have to learn which are the common sicknesses for different animals and how best to treat each one. And although most animals have similar anatomies (body parts) each animal may react differently under the same circumstance, and a vet needs to know this. Let's look at an example.

Vets need to know how each animal deals with heat, for example. They have to know that while dogs have a distinctive way of distributing heat in their bodies, letting them run longer and further than other animals – a skill that makes them excellent hunters – other animals (like rabbits) are highly sensitive when it comes to heat and can easily suffer from heatstroke. Vets need to know that a rabbit with red ears, that is panting, or that shows signs of weakness and confusion is likely overheated and needs to cool off as soon as possible.

Vets who treat household pets are always ready to give their patients vaccinations to protect them from common diseases. They also give animals special medicines to clean out their stomachs from parasites, they spay or neuter pets to control the animal population in the community, and they perform just about any type of surgery that an animal may need. Veterinarians are exceptionally good communicators, but the owner often needs special help to understand their part in helping the animal get better. The owner usually needs to provide follow up care at home for their pet. In some cases, if the veterinarian thinks that the owner is not taking proper care of their animal, they will call the authorities to make sure the animal gets the help it needs.

Other types of veterinarians don't stay in a clinic when they work – they go out to visit farms and ranches to take care of **large animals**, including sheep, horses, and cows. As you can imagine, helping a sick puppy weighing five pounds is not quite the same as helping a sick bull that weighs 1,500 pounds! These types of veterinarians have to use stronger medicines and treat different kinds of diseases and injuries. Sometimes, these vets even get to help take care of newborn horses (called "foals") and newborn cows (called "calves").

Veterinarians who work on farms and ranches have an important job, especially if the ranches they visit have animals that will later be processed into meat that is sold at stores. By keeping the animals healthy, these vets can make sure that the meat doesn't make people sick with diseases like Salmonella, E. Coli, or Mad Cow disease, all of which can kill anyone who gets them.

Still other veterinarians work in **zoos and aquariums**, where they help the animals and fish who live there to stay healthy. In the case of fish and dolphins, the veterinarians will often climb right into the tank with the patients to help them. On other occasions, they will remove the animal from the water and keep it breathing using special equipment.

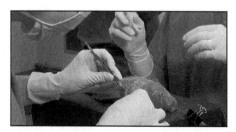

A fish can breathe out of the water during a surgery with the help of special technology[4]

These veterinarians get to work with some interesting animals, including lions, giraffes, bears, elephants, whales, dolphins, boa constrictors, penguins, crocodiles, and much more. Can you imagine going to work each day, knowing that you might get to watch a panda give birth or teach tiger cubs how to play?

Finally, some veterinarians work in the **military**. These vets may live on a base and take care of the animals of soldiers, and their families or they may go out onto the battle field and help dogs working side by side with the soldiers. Sometimes, the government even sends their military veterinarians to other countries to help control outbreaks of animal disease as part of a humanitarian mission.

No matter where they choose to work, all veterinarians do their best to make sure that each and every animal that they help gets the best treatment possible. They try to comfort the worried owner and to choose the right combination of medicine and surgery in order to treat the sickness or injury. For vets, this way of doing things is part of a lifelong career and a way for them to live up to the oath that they took when they graduated from veterinary school. In part, the oath says:

> *"Being admitted to the profession of veterinary medicine, I solemnly swear to use my scientific knowledge and skills for the benefit of society through the protection of animal health and welfare, the prevention and relief of animal suffering, the conservation of animal resources, the promotion of public health, and the advancement of medical knowledge."*

Did you see how vets promise to 'protect animal health' and to 'prevent animal suffering'? They are willing to take this vow and dedicate their lives to helping animals because they truly love animals of all shapes and sizes. Vets feel a deep compassion when they see any sort of animal suffering and want to do everything in their power to help.

For their hard work and kindness, veterinarians can expect to receive a pretty high salary. Vets who work as part of a team can expect to earn at least $50,000 to $80,000 per year, while those who own their own private clinic can take home up to $200,000 per year.

Veterinarians are remarkably special people, and no matter where they work they make a difference in the lives of the animals they help and their owners. The next time that you see a veterinarian, whether at a small clinic or at a zoo, be sure to tell them how much you appreciate the hard job that they have!

Chapter 2: What is the Training Like to Become a Veterinarian?

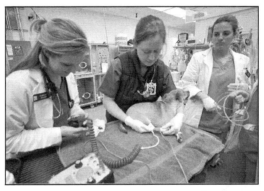

A training session at a school of veterinary medicine[5]

Those who want to become doctors of veterinary medicine must go to school for many years, just like any other kind of doctor. And although future

[5] Image source: http://tinyurl.com/lh6twwf

vets know that they will never make as much money as doctors who treat human patients or may never get as much attention, they are happy to devote so much time to studying. Why? Like Doctor Bianucci expressed in the introduction, future vets are thrilled that they will be able to earn a living doing what they love. And not just that – veterinary students want to make sure that they will become the best vet they can be. So what is the training like to become a vet? Let's find out.

The first step for a future vet is to get accepted into a **university** and to study hard to get their B.S. (Bachelor of Science) degree. To get into a good university, a future vet will need to have a good GPA (Grade Point Average) when they graduate high school and a magnificent score on their SAT (Standard Admissions Test).

Although veterinary schools will be looking at what kind of a college student the future vet is, they won't pay a whole lot of attention to the specific major that the person chooses. So most vets choose something that they feel comfortable with but that also will prepare them for the intense training of veterinary school. Some examples include Biological Sciences and Physical Sciences. The last 3 or 4 semesters will especially be looked at closely, so the last two years of college are not a time for future vets to goof off and to forget why they are there.

After graduating from a university, future veterinarians will need to take a **standardized test**, like the Graduate Record Examinations (GRE) or the Medical College Admissions test (MCAT). Both tests have section where the student must answer written and verbal questions and the GRE has a portion where the student needs to express themselves through writing.

Next, the future vet needs to get accepted in a **veterinary school**, where they will learn the specifics of caring for sick and injured animals. In the United States, there are only 28 veterinary schools that are recognized by the American Veterinary Medical Association (AVMA), which means that there is a lot of competition. In fact, it is not uncommon for only 40% of those who apply to these schools each year to be accepted. Along with a solid academic performance in college and a decent score on the standardized test, future vets must turn in an impressive application to the veterinary school that they are interested in. Whether the application is sent to a processing facility or directly to the university, the student should make it clear that they take their education seriously and are committed to becoming a good vet. They should also have at least three letters of recommendation from people who know the future vet well. For example, letters of recommendation should be obtained from the future vet's student advisor, a faculty member, and maybe a local veterinarian who knows the student well.

While they study at veterinary school (which lasts four years), students learn all about taking care of sick and injured animals. They learn subjects like anatomy, physiology (how different body parts work), biochemistry (studying chemical processes inside the body), pharmacology (how medicines treat diseases), and how to develop good communication skills. The first two years of veterinary school take place in classrooms and laboratories and focus on learning the basic science of animal care. The second two years take the future vets out into the real world, where they work with actual animals alongside experienced veterinarians, learning to identify and treat problems and diseases. They may also go out and work as part of a remarkable program called an "externship", which will take them to local animal hospitals and give them hands-on experience.

After they have graduated from their Veterinary Medical School, all that is left for a future vet is to prove their knowledge by taking yet **another standardized test**, called the North American Veterinary Licensing Exam, which is made up of 360 multiple choice questions. After having passed this test, the students will receive their Doctor of Veterinary Medicine (DVM) degree, officially making them veterinarians!

Most states require **certain certifying exams** to make sure the doctor really knows what they are doing, after which the veterinary doctor can treat animals anywhere in the state. The doctor may choose to open their own small clinic, to work as part of a team in a larger animal hospital, to visit farms and ranches, to work at a zoo or aquarium, to join the military, or even to teach at a university or veterinary school.

Although most of their time will be spent taking care of animals at their new jobs, veterinarians must continue to receive education about new technologies and may even be required to take tests every now and then to prove that they are still qualified doctors.

After you have seen all of the intense training that a veterinarian has to complete, are you still interested in this career? Are you willing to work hard to get the scholarships you'll need and maybe even go into some debt to pay for your education? If so, then it would seem that you are really committed to this job and that you are ready to learn more.

Now, let's find out a little about the working conditions of veterinarians in the next section.

Chapter 3: Is Being a Veterinarian An Easy job?

Veterinarians sometimes have to work with extremely dangerous animals, like this rhinoceros[6]

Veterinarians never quite know what their day is going to be like when they show up for work. While they schedule appointments with patients

[6] Image source: http://www.scotsman.com/news/what-does-it-take-to-train-dangerous-animals-at-edinburgh-zoo-1-2560807

like other medical doctors do, they also know that they may have to deal with emergencies and unexpected reactions from the animals that they work with. In this section, we will see some of the common working conditions that can make being a veterinarian a somewhat challenging job.

Being available to work 24 hours a day. At most jobs, employees have to be at work by a certain time and can go home at a certain time. For example, many people who work in large office buildings have to be at their desks by 9 AM every morning. They work until 12:00 PM or so, take an hour for lunch, and then go back to work until 5 PM. At five o'clock sharp, most office workers can simply turn off their computers and go home, with no questions asked. Any work that they haven't finished can wait until the next day.

But for a veterinarian, life is a little different. For example, a veterinarian that owns a small clinic will have regular office hours, perhaps from 9-5. But if they are in the middle of treating a sick animal or performing a surgery and they realize that it is time to go to lunch or to go home, do you think that the veterinarian can just drop what they are doing and leave? Of course not! Veterinarians must finish whatever they have started, even if it means that they have to work late into the night on a complicated surgery or treatment.

In addition, many veterinarians must be prepared 24 hours a day to work at a moment's notice. After all, sometimes animals get sick or are injured in the middle of the night or during the weekend. In cases like that, veterinarians must be prepared to go right away either to their clinic or to the home of the animal to give it emergency medical attention. Can you imagine knowing that, at any second, your phone might ring, and you might have to stop what you're doing to go to work?

Working with dangerous animals. As we saw in the picture at the beginning of this section, some veterinarians have to work with dangerous animals as part of their job. They may have to check the teeth of a lion, trim the nails of a bear, or cure an eye problem in a rhinoceros. How can the vets avoid getting injured with working with such strong and often aggressive patients?

Many animals in zoos have been touched by humans since they were babies and are used to getting shots and checkups. But in the case of some animals that may have had some terrible experiences in the past, vets can't go near them without risking injury. If the animal needs a surgery, then the vet must find a way to approach the animal without getting hurt.

In such cases, the vets have to give the animal a special injection (called a tranquilizer) that will make it go to sleep. Then, they can go into the animal's area and either treat it right there or take it to a specific medical area. They must work quickly to give the animal a checkup and to treat any problems before it wakes up. By the time the animal is awake, the problem will be treated, and it can go back to its life as normal.

A particular challenge comes up when zoo vets need to vaccinate newborn animals, like lion cubs. How can they get to the cubs without the mother, who is highly protective, hurting the doctors? At the Paignton Zoo in the United Kingdom, zookeepers had to shut the mother in her den and keep her away from her babies for a few minutes while a team of five, wearing big leather gloves, moved in. The team checked the heartbeat of the cubs, gave them their medicine, and weighed them. Then, they left the lion enclosure, let the mother go, and reunited the family. Although they try not to touch the animals too much, the vets admit that it is exciting to be able to hold the cubs and be so close to them.

A zoo vet holds a lion cub at the Paignton Zoo[7]

But zoo vets can never forget that they are working with potentially dangerous animals, and even young animals (like cubs) have teeth and claws that can do some real damage.

Communicating with the owner of an animal.

Just like parents who have to take care of their small children that are too young to take care of themselves, pet owners must make good

---

[7] Image source: http://www.paigntonzoo.org.uk/news/details/how-to-vaccinate-a-lion-cub

decisions when it comes to the health of their animals. At the end of the day, they are the ones responsible for making sure that their pet eats the right food, gets enough exercise, is protected against common diseases, and receives treatment for any sicknesses or injuries. However, not all pet owners are as responsible as they should be.

When owners bring their animals to a veterinarian, they are taking a terrific first step. But some owners are so worried and so emotional that the vet often has a hard time explaining what the owner needs to do to help their pet. Sometimes, the vet has to wait a few minutes before giving the owner any specific instructions to make sure that the owner is calm and under control. For example, after a major surgery (like to remove a cancerous tumor), some animals need unique treatment which may include taking medicine at certain times of the day and having their bandages changed. When the vet tries to explain all this to the owner, it can be difficult if the owner isn't paying attention or is very emotional.

Vets can only do so much while the animal is under their care - the rest is up to the owner. So imagine how challenging it can be sometimes to speak with an owner that may or may not do what you tell them to!

Managing a business. Along with all of the unique challenges that we have mentioned so far, many veterinarians must also deal with the stress of running a business. 66% of vets work in private practice, and about two-thirds of those (about 37,000 vets in 2006) work mainly with "companion animals", or pets. Most of these 37,000 vets work in small clinics spread out across the country, and many of them are the owners of the clinic.

When they aren't worrying about treating the patients who come to see them, many vets have to worry about the day-to-day concerns that come with owning and running a business. They have to make sure that all of their employees are happy and productive, that there are enough supplies in the clinic, that the electrical bill is paid, that insurance is enough to protect everyone working there, that clients don't get angry and sue the vet, and so on. It's almost as if some vets have to deal with the stress from two jobs – being a veterinary doctor *and* being a small business owner.

However, despite the challenges that come with the job, being a vet is not all stress and challenges. Most of the time, it is an extremely rewarding career that thousands of vets around the world are happy to practice. Let's learn more about the daily routine of a veterinarian in the next section.

What is an average day like for a veterinarian?

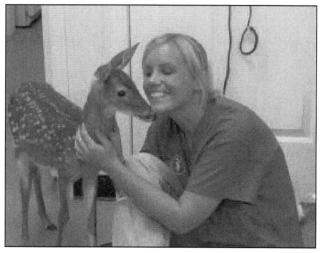

A veterinary assistant working with a fawn (a baby deer)[8]

As we saw earlier, each day at work is different for a veterinarian. They may have to deal with emergencies, travel to treat a patient, perform a surgery, a vaccination, or a checkup – all in the same day. So even though it can be hard to predict what they may be doing on any given

---

[8] Image source: http://careertrove.org/veterinary-assistant-salary/

day, let's have a look at a sample description of one vet's daily activities, as written in his journal:

<u>MONDAY SEPTEMBER 16</u>

8:30 AM - Travel to work. *After getting up and having breakfast, I headed out the door and tried to be to work by 9 AM, the time my animal care center opens for business and the first patients start arriving.*

9:00 AM - First appointment: Vaccination for a six week old puppy. *The owner brought in her small black Labrador retriever puppy that needs to receive its first set of vaccinations. These vaccinations will protect the puppy against common diseases like Distemper, measles, parainfluenza, and Bordatella.*

9:15 AM – Second appointment: Neutering a male cat. *The owner was concerned that his cat will wander around and raise the wild cat* *population too much, so he asked us to neuter his cat (remove the reproductive parts). The male cat, about seven months old, was put under general anesthesia, which meant that it was knocked out for the surgery. After the cat fell asleep, we made two small cuts above the scrotum removed and each testicle. Then we tied the cords to stop the bleeding. The whole surgery only took about ten minutes to perform. After the surgery, the cat was moved to an area where it will rest and recover for two or three hours.*

9:45 AM – Unscheduled walk-in patient: Dehydrated rabbit. *The owner brought in a young rabbit whose ears were dropping, and skin was not flexible because of dehydration. I used a plastic syringe to spray a special fluid into the rabbit's mouth, being careful not to force the liquid down the throat (which could make the animal choke). I also sprayed the bunny's ears with cool water to reduce its body temperature.*

The owner was told that the bunny should stay at the vet's office for 48 hours so it could be observed and to make sure there weren't any lasting effects from the dehydration.

10:00 AM – Third appointment: Question about feeding schedule for a boa constrictor. *The owner had recently purchased a boa constrictor from a local pet store and wanted to know how often they should feed it and with what kind of food. I explained to the owner that boa constrictors, like other types of serpents, prefer to eat live rodents like small mice. Depending on the age of the snake, the owner could purchase baby or adult mice, and should feed the snake at least once per week. I recommended that the owner should return as soon as possible with the actual snake so I could see its size and health and thus decide how much it should be eating.*

10:15 AM – Fourth appointment: A very old dog with bone cancer. *The owner, who has been* visiting me for many years, is worried about his old dog - a German shepherd named "Scout". Scout is thirteen years old and for some time has been fighting against a type of cancer that seems to be spreading. He has already had three expensive surgeries, and Scout's owner is worried that the animal is still in a great deal of pain. I explained that most German shepherds do not live much more than thirteen years and that there is not much more that I can do to alleviate Scout's pain and suffering. The owner asked me if it is time to put Scout to sleep and to let him die peacefully. I answered that, while it is a personal matter, it would probably be the kindest thing to do. After giving the owner a few minutes to say goodbye to his cherished pet of thirteen years, I gave Scout a drug to make him sleepy and then gave him another injection that slowly stopped his heart. Although both the owner and I knew that it was the right thing to do, we were both sad. The owner took his dog home to bury it on his property.

10:45 AM – Check up on animals in the kennel.
In my clinic, I have a special area where all kinds of animals recover from surgery and get some rest. While there, they are cared for by a team of professionals. A few times per day, I go to this area and make sure that each of the animals is having its needs looked after. I spent some seeing how my team was caring for them and gave them a few suggestions and answered some questions they had.

11:30 AM-12:30 PM –LUNCH

12:30 PM – Unscheduled walk-in patient: Abandoned baby deer found on property. *A retired couple came in and explained that they found an abandoned baby deer (a fawn) on their property. It seems like the mother was hit by a truck while crossing the road and that somehow the baby managed to escape. The fawn went into the couple's garden and got trapped in the* fence. They freed it and brought it to the vet to see what they should do. I told them that, while it was good that they wanted to help, they should have left the fawn alone and called Animal Control. But now that the deer was here, I would make sure it was fed and then I would call Animal Control myself. The fawn would be taken to a special habitat where it would be taken care of for a few months and then released back into the wild.

1:00 PM – Last appointment: Cystotomy in male cat to remove bladder stones. *Last week, an owner brought in her male cat that was urinating blood. X-rays showed that the cat had several small stones in his bladder that would need to be removed through a "Cystotomy", which is a surgery where the bladder is opened and the stones are removed. Today was the day of the surgery. The cat was knocked out to protect it from the pain of the surgery and to relax its muscles. Then a small incision was made near* the bladder, the stones were removed, and then the opening was sewn shut. The cat woke up a couple of hours later and can probably go home tomorrow. It will need two weeks of rest until it completely recovers. The whole surgery took about one and a half hours.

2:30 PM – Spent some time in office looking at test results from previous week and trying to diagnose various symptoms. *Just like doctors who work with human patients, veterinarians often have to spend time researching and thinking about difficult cases before they can recommend any sort of medicine or treatment. I try to schedule time so that I'm not hurried when making these decisions.*

4:00 PM – No more appointments, was able to go home early. *Although it is not too common, sometimes I get to go home a little early. After all, I know that I am going to be "on call", which means that I have to be ready to go back to work* *at a moment's notice. After I leave my clinic, I spent some time with my family and did some chores around the house.*

Wow! Isn't it amazing to see how many different types of patients a vet must deal with and how crazy their daily schedule can be sometimes? Does it make you appreciate how hard these men and women work each and every day?

Chapter 4: What is the Hardest Part of Being a Veterinarian?

As you can see, veterinarians have challenging and busy lives. Each day brings new opportunities to put into practice all that they have learned. But what is the most difficult part of being a vet? It has to do with the **unpredictable reactions** of the animals that they are trying to help. Let's learn more.

Each animal, like each person, has a distinct personality. An animal's personality may be shaped by how people have treated it and even by its genetic background. For example, German shepherds are known to be highly intelligent and trainable dogs, while Labradors have the reputation of being very loving and loyal. What does this variety of personality in the animal kingdom mean for a vet?

Just like some people are easier to get along with than others, or get sick more often than others, not all animals react the same when they go to the vet. Some are remarkably calm while others get scared and fight. Some respond very well to medicine while others only get sicker and sicker. How do these unpredictable reactions affect a vet?

On occasion, an animal suddenly becomes aggressive and **attacks** the vet. Depending on the animal, this may or may not be dangerous. An angry cat may surprise a vet or scratch them, but it will not likely do any serious damage. However, in the case of zoo vets working with larger animals, things can quickly become much more dangerous. Let's see an example.

On May 24, 2013, zookeeper Sarah McClay was attacked by a Sumatran tiger in a British zoo. She entered the enclosure at 4 PM, and a ten year-old tiger, who had been at the zoo since he was a cub, attacked her. Sarah later died at a hospital from her injuries. While she was not a trained veterinarian, Sarah was an expert at working with big cats. The attack surprised her, and she didn't actually have a chance to run away. Can you understand how even an experienced vet may be worried sometimes when they have to work with certain animals?

The best way that vets can protect themselves is to never work alone and to take every safety precaution that they can. For example, before checking up on some big cats, some zoos tranquilize them to make sure the cat can't hurt anyone.

Another unexpected reaction is when an animal gets so sick that the vet must put it to sleep (a process called *euthanasia*). Some animals, no matter how much their owners love them and no matter how much treatment they give them, just don't get better. Sometimes a bad injury (like getting hit by a car) has done too much damage; sometimes cancer spreads throughout the whole body, or sometimes the animal is just plain old. Sometimes, veterinarians feel that the best way to live up to their oath of providing "relief of animal suffering" is to give the animal a mixture of chemicals that will make it fall asleep and stop its heart from beating.

Most of the time, the owner is the one who will recognize that the animal is suffering, but often the vet has to be the strong one and suggest euthanasia. Can you imagine telling a person that there is nothing more you can do for their beloved pet? Vets love animals and have dedicated their lives towards making animals feel better and giving them better lives. As you can imagine, suggesting and carrying out euthanasia can be one of the hardest parts of being a vet. So how can vets deal with the pain of having to put an animal that is suffering to sleep?

T. J. Dunn, Jr., who is an experienced veterinarian, wrote: "No one is comfortable with death, especially your veterinarian and animal hospital staff who face death every day."[9] Vets are sad when an animal is euthanized, but they are happy knowing that the animal won't be suffering anymore. And it helps owners to know that it's okay to cry when saying goodbye to a longtime companion.

Do you think that you could deal with these unpredictable reactions of animals?

---

[9] Quotation source: http://www.petmd.com/dog/care/evr_dg_euthanasia_what_to_expect#.UjozWMaUS71

Chapter 5: What Does the Future Hold for the Career of a Veterinarian?

In ten years or so, maybe around the time that you will be graduating from college and looking for work, will there be a lot of veterinary jobs available? Yes, there absolutely will be.

According to the US Bureau of Labor and Statistics[10], jobs requiring a doctorate degree are expected to grow by 20% in the next few years while veterinarian jobs in particular are expected to grow by 36%. That means that being a veterinarian will be a hugely in-demand job in the future. Vets will be able to find jobs taking care

---

[10] Information source: http://www.bls.gov/ooh/healthcare/veterinarians.htm

of small animals, helping to regulate animal health in the food industry, or even teaching at one of the many veterinary schools of medicine.

Veterinarians will also be using exciting new technologies in the future to make them even more effective at their jobs. The new machines and techniques that are currently being used on human patients may one day be used to make surgeries safer and less painful for dogs, cats, horses, cows, and just about every other animal. What kind of technology might you work with in the future if you decide to become a vet?

Laser lithotripsy: The Ohio State University Veterinary Medical Center has recently acquired a piece of technology that may soon be used around the country. Using laser technology, vets can break up kidney stones (which are particularly common in dogs and usually require a surgery). If the laser manages to break down the stones, then the dog may be able to just get rid of them through urination and avoid a potentially painful (and expensive) surgery.

Non-invasive surgery: In humans, doctors have recently started to perform complicated surgeries using very small incisions. For example, they can replace a heart valve in a human patient by opening a small hole in the patient's thigh and pushing small tools up through a major artery all the way to the heart, reducing recovery time and trauma to the patient. Vets hope that, in the future, similar ideas can be used to replace valves on older dogs without having to cut open their chest. This would save both time and money and would help the dog to recover more quickly.

Acoustic emission data: Horses (especially racehorses) sometimes get extremely small fractures in their leg bones that can be terribly hard to detect. After a day of heavy training or running in a race, these small fractures can make leg bones break and the horse may end up falling or even dying. So veterinarians everywhere were excited to hear about a new technology that was being tested out that uses acoustic emission data (sound waves) to detect even small cracks in a horse's bones. If vets can find these small fractures in time, they will know that the horse needs plenty of rest and time to heal, and thus the horse can avoid having a serious fall or dying.

The future is bright for the career of a vet. In the next ten years or so, there will be plenty of jobs and lots of exciting new technology to use.

Chapter 6: How Can You Get Ready Now to Become a Veterinarian?

Lexie Fletcher wants to become a veterinarian when she grows up[11]

In order to go to veterinary school, you need to have graduated from college, which means you probably can't think too seriously about applying yet. But while you are waiting for time to pass

[11] Image source: http://www.annarbor.com/pets/ask-the-veterinarian/

and getting ready for college, there are lots of things that you can do to prepare yourself for a career as a veterinarian. Let's have a look at a few practical skills that you can work on developing right now that will help you out later on.

Learn to love math, chemistry, and biology. As we saw earlier, the training to become a veterinarian involves lots of math and science. So learn now to love these subjects and to understand them well. In the future, as a veterinarian, you will have to understand how different medicines work, how to treat different animals with problems in different parts of their bodies, and how to change the dosage of a medicine or drug according to the size of the animal. Without an advanced knowledge of science and math, you accidentally may end up hurting an animal instead of helping it.

Volunteer in your community. Most veterinary schools won't accept any students unless they have spent many hours volunteering with a local vet or at an animal shelter or farm. But it's not just about filling a space on an application – when you volunteer, you should do so to learn as much as you can and to get a real idea of what working with animals for a living is all about. Take advantage and as the experts as many questions as you can.

Show compassion and love for animals. A veterinarian, above all else, needs to be an animal lover. No matter what kind of veterinarian you end up being, you should undoubtedly have affection and respect for the animal patients that you will be treating. This can help you to stay motivated on the tough days and will make sure that your decisions are always in the best interests of the patient.

Develop critical thinking skills. Vets sometimes need to diagnose strange diseases or find a way to carry out a complicated surgery. In situations like that, they need to use critical thinking skills. What are "critical thinking skills"? Critical thinking is a thought process where the focus is on logic and not on emotion. In other words, no matter how much stress the vet feels or how emotional the owner may be, the vet has a special responsibility to be the one to think calmly and to find the best solution to the animal's problem. Start learning this particular skill now. You can practice critical thinking when doing homework, fixing a car, or even when listening as a friend tells you a problem.

Learn how to be a leader. As we saw earlier, a large number of vets in the United States work at small clinics, and many of them are the owners of their clinics. This can bring a great amount of satisfaction and freedom – but it can also bring some stress. A good vet also has to be a good leader, a person who can give instructions to their employees and who can make sure that everyone is happy at their job. Learn the valuable skills of being a leader now, perhaps by joining a sports team or a club at school. If you can stay calm and communicate clearly even when moments are tense, it will help you when directing a group of employees later on.

Conclusion

A veterinarian with a patient[12]

Wow! We have learned a lot about the fascinating career of a veterinarian. What was your favorite part? Was it when we learned about how many types of vets are out there working? Or was it when we saw the new technology that vets might be using in the

---

[12] Image source: http://coast2coastrx.com/index.php/more-benefits/discount-veterinary-services

future? Let's review some of the most pivotal points that we learned so that you don't forget them.

The first section told us what it is that veterinarians do all day and what different kinds of veterinarians you can expect to meet. Basically, we saw that all veterinarians focus on helping sick and injured animals to feel better and that you may see one hard at work in a zoo, teaching at a university, or working in a small clinic. We also saw the oath that all veterinarians must take – the one where they promise to do everything in their power to improve the lives of their animal patients.

The second section showed us what the training is like to become a veterinarian. After going to college, did you know that vets have to go to a particular medical school, just like doctors that work with human patients? We saw that vets have to go to about eight years of college and pass lots and lots of tests before they can begin practicing medicine on their animal patients.

The third section answered the question: "Is being a vet an easy job?" There can be no doubt that the answer to that question is "no". We saw that being a vet has some truly unique challenges each and every day, including working with dangerous animals, being on call 24 hours a day, communicating with pet owners, and managing the employees at a small clinic. However, despite the challenges, vets love what they do and they love helping animals.

The fourth section showed us what the average day of work is like for a veterinarian. Did you like looking over the shoulder of a vet as he went through his daily activities? It was interesting to see how a doctor of veterinary medicine spends his time just like any other doctor does: handling emergencies, visiting patients, researching, performing surgeries, and talking with family members.

The fifth section told us what the hardest part of being a vet is: dealing with the unpredictable reactions of animals. Sometimes a vet has to be ready to deal with an animal that becomes aggressive, and in the case of large animals (like tigers) the vet's very life may even be in danger. We also saw how vets must deal with animals that are sick and suffering. Sometimes the owner and the vet decide that the kindest thing to do is to euthanize the animal, even though it makes everybody terribly sad.

The sixth section talked about what the future holds for veterinarians. We saw that, in ten years or so, there will be lots of jobs available for veterinarians and that they will be working with some highly advanced technology. Can you imagine using special tools to see small fractures in a horse's leg or to break up kidney stones in a suffering dog? The new technology will be exciting and will allow vets to help more and more animals to live happy and healthy lives.

Finally, the seventh section told you what you can do right now to get ready to be a veterinarian. Even though you may still have to wait a few years before going to college and then to veterinary school, there are some fundamental qualities and skills that you can learn right now that will help you to be a good vet. Do you remember the qualities that you should develop? We saw the need to: learn to love math and science; to volunteer; to show compassion for animals; to practice critical thinking, and to learn how to be a leader. Which one of these qualities will you start working on first?

The career of a veterinarian doesn't just help families to care for their animals – it helps communities to have healthy food and keeps diseases from spreading. We can be so thankful to the men and women who work hard to take care of sick and injured animals. Why not say "thank you" the next time you see a veterinarian?

19303965R00040

Made in the USA
Middletown, DE
13 April 2015